Grá

Erin O'Donoghue

BookLeaf Publishing

Presentation by *BookLeaf Publishing*

Web: www.bookleafpub.com

E-mail: info@bookleafpub.com

ISBN: 9789357610902

First edition 2022

DEDICATION

To Shane.

To Sempai Dad and Shihan Mum.

To Michael, Donna and Bianca.

To Mammy and Ping.

To all my Murri/Koori/Yolngu mobs out there.

I love you all dearly.

ACKNOWLEDGEMENT

I would like to acknowledge the traditional owners of this land. Australia will always be Aboriginal Country.

Thank you to all the brave mob that have come before me. I will continue your fight; no matter the cost.

Her Shrouded Head

Life is blooming,
Life is looming.
Her head pokes over,
Nosy, intrusive, unwelcome.
Her head is cloaked.
Demon like.
Swiftly grasping anything bright!
Why? You ask why?
There's no reason, only sorrow.
Life is blooming,
no need for darkness.
It needs no reason,
only a victim.
'But life is blooming,' I say.
'Everything is good! I'm grateful!'
'Doesn't matter...' the Demon replies.
'You're under my spell;
You are my victim. Forever shrouded.
I need your outlook to be clouded.
For here is where I survive in your doom!'
'No!' I shriek.
'I won't live in gloom!'
I slash and fight her shrouded head.
It's forever gone, my depression is dead.

The Fighter

The date emerges,
my skin tingles.
All my training is tested,
I'm sick to my core like shingles.

Sweat is the answer,
sweat is the key.
Just Kiai louder,
It's easy...see?

Nerves in my throat,
I hear my name called.
I'm in the warm up room,
my legs sprawled.

"It's time," he says.
My focus begins to clear,
For this moment
is why I'm here.

Gloves are off,
mouthguard in place.
I must take it steady
it's a fight not a race.

"Hajime!" The ref cries,
begin, start, fight!
She lands the first blow,
my mind is in plight.

My heart flickers
the danger is near
I concentrate on my training
not on the fear.

"Move Erin, make her pay!"
I barely hear the side line
Yet move instinctively out of the way.

"Now!" he yelps,
As we've done before.
My foot finds her face
Her body hits the floor.

It's done, it's finished
My fear has gone.
Pride takes its place
A new trophy in its case.

"Osu!" I cry, more from relief
It's done, her trainer in disbelief.

For now I am champion,
From the ashes I rose.

Who would of thought,
not you I suppose?

Perfection is Free

I look in the mirror, what do I see?
A scar, a freckle, some pimples...
Nothing is perfect, perfection is free.
A simple concept; deceptively.
the sun is never that bright,
the grass never that green.
Her skin isn't smooth or pristine.

Swiping left, swiping right,
Catching an action mid flight.
None of it is real, don't you see?
Nothing is perfect, perfection is free.

Lives in a bubble, flawless and fake,
fooling all followers a risk you take.
What if they saw my life for what it is?
Something real...visceral...complicated.

The smile across my face hides my tears,
Increasing inadequacy strengthens my fears.
Who would love such things?
The scar, the freckle, the pimples?
I have to hide these things don't you see?
Nothing is perfect, perfection is free.

The Small Crocodile

Beware! Beware!
Do not stand there!

It's rife with trouble,
the longer you stay in a bubble!

Hide! Hide!
Your eyes should be wide!

No one to trust,
keeping low is a must.

The "Crocodiles" are waiting,
Their clever language baiting.

This room isn't safe,
Her eyes surveyed the place.

For I am the 'Small Crocodile',
I've been here for quite a while.

These other Crocs are not what they seem,
Listen to your Dad's dream!

For these Crocs you are a threat,

Move now or forever regret.

The Trees, she says
Make that your new address.

I'll keep 'swimming' here
Hide now while it's clear.

For I am the Small Crocodile
My number is one you can always dial.

My goal is to not let them win,
Wiping away their Crocodile grin

Not all Crocs are like me
If you stay, you'll soon see

So move! Move now!
Use a boat, oar or dow.

Hiding now she is ok,
Thanks to the Small Crocodile, who saved the day.

These are the words I've heard

You're incompetent!
Why are you this stupid?
You'd look pretty with your hair down.

These are the words I've heard.

I normally don't date fat chicks,
You're a loser with no future.
No one will love you.

These are the words I've heard.

Is there something wrong with your body?
You are overweight.
You'd be so much prettier if you did A...B...C...

These are the words I've heard.

But it's not all bad.
Sometimes the words are good.
Sometimes the words are accepting, supportive and nice.

These words have shaped me.
Challenged me.
Made me grow.

For all these words have come from men.
Men who think they have a hold over my life.
For some reason, I am a threat to these men.

These are the words I've heard.

It took a long time for the words to change:
I'm proud of you.
You're beautiful.
You're intelligent and
I love you.

These are the words I've heard.

The people who bring you down
are the cowards of this world.
The people who have no conviction.
The people who are drowning in their own
hearts.

These are the words I've heard.

The words changed when I met someone new.
A man who had nice words,
Had a kind heart.

Wait for the man who lifts you up.

These are the words I've heard.

My Wedding Vow

Our story begins in an Irish Bar,
The irony of this can only take us so far,
Cause the man I met in the bar that night,
turned out to be my Mr Right.

For the man who stands before me now,
has held my hand and kissed my brow.
Through the good things and the bad,
He's the closest friend I've ever had.

Four years of laughter, four years of joy;
is more than I ever expected from this Irish boy.

To say I love you, is not enough;
Cause love only covers the 'airy-fairy' stuff.

Because I respect, adore, admire everything you do,
And truly appreciate the sacrifices you've made for me and you.

You've made me the happiest I ever thought I could be,
together building our little family of 3 (now four!)

I stand here now ecstatic, my heart bursting at the seams;
because becoming your wife fulfils my dreams.
So if you let me, from this day,
I promise forever, to make you feel the same way. 4

Choice of the Womb

I'm free at last!
Breaking away from my past.
You don't have to linger there,
I never knew, I always lived in despair.
Now with a partner,
my prospects high.
I'll never need to pursue another guy.
Oh the relief of a wedding ring,
My soul is happy; what joy it brings.
To move to the next chapter of my life,
now that I'm the role of wife.
You're thinking of children, yes?
Children for most would be best.
I do not share this view with the world
My husband agrees,
a baby of fur I do prefer.
But not just one two, or three,
Four is the number for me.
Such courage it takes to seize a life you want.
Some many steal your 'pen'
Even try and choose the font.
I draw my life how I please
For it's me that must live it.
Quite simply I deliver it.
Why does the object of my womb hurt so many?

Do they not see my sorrow and gloom?
That life is not for all
that life is also not mine to judge;
so you choose whichever gives you the sweeter fudge.
I have an affinity for animals,
their love, their spirit, their charm.
For they in my life do me no harm.
So happy we are!
People do detest.
They don't understand this suits me best.

B

Twinkle twinkle, little B star,
what a talent that you are.
All above the world so bright,
Can't wait to see your name in light.

Twinkle twinkle little B star,
What a world you've created thus far.
17 and on the straight,
To have glitz and glamour - we can't wait!

Twinkle twinkle little B star
Thanks for being the best niece by far.
Love you with all our might,
Keep shining, shining ever so bright!

Twinkle twinkle little B star
Thanks for being who you are xoxxoxoxoxo

Moneeza

Her eyes were shiny and brown.
Big and wide.
Her skin clear;
Her hijab a matter of pride.

The portal around her face,
gave away such beauty and grace.

She was my first Muslim friend.
Moneeza.

Islamaphobia, something I don't see,
How can people have such hatred?
Why toward her instead of me?

What has she done to you?
Or to your way of life?
Her heart is pure,
A guiding light in my life.

She was my first Muslim friend,
and she wasn't the last.
The nation needs to move forward,
not focus on the past.

She was my first Muslim friend,
I'll never forget.
I miss working with her,
her laugh and smile was always set.

Thank you Moneeza,
for opening my eyes.
I just wish the rest of the world,
would stop these phobic horrible lies.

Grá

Pronounced GRAW,
It's an Irish word for LOVE.

The Emerald Isle,
The green rolling hills.

I love its people,
I love its food.

It's just shame its so far away.

An Ode to Buglette

Fluffy ears,
Brown eyes that flutter
She's cute as a button
Not lamb dressed as mutton.

Such a beautiful girl,
My life is complete
How did we survive thus far;
Without you at my feet?

Running, jumping
Tearing the place apart,
It doesn't matter
You live in my heart.

The 'Destructor'
The 'Sucky Calf'
It doesn't matter
You're my better half.

We love you Buglette,
So grateful to have you here
Such a menagerie we make
Making me smile from ear to ear!

Circles

The circles are tight,
The circles are many,
I really need a friend,
But don't see any.

The circles are tight,
The circles have power;
All white and superior
In their Ivory Tower.

The circles are tight,
The circles are lying;
Leaving me out
I feel like I'm dying.

The circles are tight,
The circles spread far;
If only they had colour
They could raise their bar.

The circles are tight,
The circles are similar;
I stand on the side,
Nothing in them familiar.

The circles are tight,
The circles are there;
I’ll never let them win,
As long as I’m aware.

Colours

White? Black?
What does this mean?
I am both,
But this is not seen.

Don't judge me,
Like a book cover;
I have walked both sides,
Over concrete and clover.

This is my power,
To see and live both ways;
Many don't realise
This is my way out of the frey.

Its like tea they say,
No matter the milk
Your skin colour doesn't matter
All colours make nice silk

I hope the future is together,
A sea of black, white and brindle;
And I want to see more people like me
Their culture rekindled.

Heavy Doors

Heavy doors,
Loud voices.
Locked in a cage,
Result of bad choices.

Lacking in space,
assigned to cells.
Forming lines on their face,
This school has radios not bells.

Young and all creeds,
Mothering teens,
Penances paid for their bad deeds.

The Little Black Duck

Kind, humble and fierce;
His love for us unyielding;
His brown eyes unfold and pierce.

Strong, black and deadly;
In more ways than one,
Lots of smiles,
And plenty of fun.

A beer in one hand
And a rod in the other.
The eyes rolling behind him
Of my doting, loyal mother.

Loves to fish,
But not to swim.
He rather enjoys archery,
Karate or kickboxing – that's for him.

A mentor and confidant,
A man that tells the truth;
He's my best mate,
A research assistant – a common sleuth.

So many things he is to me,

So many things he is to others;
He's my protective Dad,
But not one that smothers.

My favourite saying,
From our history – his wit and humour
Something he's taught to me.

If you haven't heard, you're sure out of luck,
To not know Phil – the Little Black Duck.

The One They Call Sue

Loud and strong
but stubborn to a fault
She laughs heartily,
Brings anything to a halt.

She is the protector,
the one we call Sue.
She is our Matriarch
The only mum I knew.

A clenched fist,
and an iron heart.
She's given many students
their flying start.

Compassionate? Yes!
Fiery? Yes!
She only wants what's best!

I respect her,
Love her,
Admire her!

She is my mother,

the one they call Sue.

Welcome to Sikles

Cold and foreboding,
but intriguing all the same.
I've come here to discover,
not relish in fame.

Snow capped, isolated.
Scary yet true,
Its a test between me and you.

Brown faces smile,
Hands clasping together.
NAMASTE!
Wishing us foreigners a safe stay.

Poor community
But open hearts,
They don't need cars
Their legs take them far.

Yuppie guilt consumes me,
gratitude for my home,
Yet I'm jealous
of all the unturned stone.

Simple and happy

Free to roam
I can see why
They call this place home.

The air is fresh,
Cold yet warm.
I miss my own bed
but am not forlorn.

Jam! Jam! They cry!
Let's go, it means,
They smile as they instruct,
No one is left to lean.

One foot in front of the other,
I sweat and I curse
Its one big mountain,
Its a giant f*cker!

We've made it now,
to our oasis!
Sikles its called,
The place with shiny, happy faces.

True Reconciliation

We need blackfellas at the top,
We need blackfellas in charge.
No more white superiority,
I want more black folk to call Sarge.

Its getting better,
but there's still a way to go.
Nothing will move
If you don't say so.

Vote Yes!
Stand up!
Speak up!
Show up!

Our voice will be heard,
Together we must unite,
it can't be just us
in this fight.

Australia, young and free
but only for faces
That are creamy and white like me.

Its not fair.

Its been 200 years,
How many more false agreements?
How many more false fears?

A voice is needed,
A voice is here,
Stop focusing on those
That have never had fear.

To the people we run
The vote will be soon
Lets all band together,
The new age has begun.

www.ingramcontent.com/pod-product-compliance
Lightning Source LLC
Chambersburg PA
CBHW062204160726
48282CB00027B/988
* 9 7 8 9 3 5 7 6 1 0 9 0 2 *